Trap Street

TRAP STREET

POEMS BY
Will Cordeiro

WINNER OF THE 2019 ABLE MUSE BOOK AWARD

ABLE MUSE PRESS

Able Muse Press

www.ablemusepress.com

Printed in the United States of America

Library of Congress Cataloging-in-Publication Data

Names: Cordeiro, Will, 1979- author.
Title: Trap street / poems by Will Cordeiro.
Description: San Jose, CA : Able Muse Press, 2021.
Identifiers: LCCN 2019059802 (print) | LCCN 2019059803 (ebook) | ISBN
9781773490571 (paperback) | ISBN 9781773490588 (digital)
Subjects: LCGFT: Poetry.
Classification: LCC PS3603.O7342246 T73 2021 (print) | LCC PS3603.O7342246
(ebook) | DDC 811/.6--dc23
LC record available at https://lccn.loc.gov/2019059802
LC ebook record available at https://lccn.loc.gov/2019059803

Cover image: *Earthships and Their Neighbors*, 2005
    Lisa Sanditz
    American, born 1973
    Acrylic on canvas
    Collection of the Herbert F. Johnson Museum of Art, Cornell University
    Acquired through the generosity of Helen Appel, Class of 1955, and
    Robert J. Appel, Class of 1953; 2006.007
    Image courtesy of the Johnson Museum

Cover & book design by Alexander Pepple

Will Cordeiro photo (on page 109) by Benjamin Garcia

Able Muse Press is an imprint of *Able Muse: A Review of Poetry, Prose & Art*—at
www.ablemuse.com

Able Muse Press
467 Saratoga Avenue #602
San Jose, CA 95129

for M. S. Coe

Acknowledgments

My grateful acknowledgments go to the editors of the following publications where these poems, some in earlier versions, first appeared:

Best New Poets 2016: "Open Country"

Blue Earth Review: "Arroyo"

Boxcar Poetry Review: "Daylight Savings"

Brooklyner: "At the Wheel" (as "Long Drive Home") and "Aubade, Provincetown"

burnt district: "Fatalist" and "Origin"

Cimarron Review: "Umbra Season"

The Cincinnati Review: "Fairy Tale"

Copper Nickel: "Route 66, Petrified Forest" and "Nizohni Point"

Crab Orchard Review: "Ephemerata" and "Provinceland"

Fifth Wednesday Journal: "Evening"

Flyway: A Journal of Writing and Environment: "Vistas"

Fourteen Hills: "August, Rehoboth Beach" and "Pay Phone"

Harpur Palate: "Terminal"

Innisfree Poetry Journal: "Half Sister"

Jackson Hole Review: "Hawk Song"

Juke Joint: "Hay Bucking" and "Homecoming"

Memoir Journal: "Brother's Keeper"

Museum of Americana: "Manifest Destiny"

National Poetry Review: "Dune Maze"

New Walk: "Mirage"

Other Poetry: "My hometown"

[PANK]: "Landscape with Bureaucracy and Owl" and "Cenotaph"

Phoebe: "Homeward Under Falling Stars"

Poecology: "Cavities and Conduits" (as "Basin Journal")

Poetry Northwest: "Inclemency"

Requited: "Fractures"

The Rush: "Death of a Code Talker"

Salamander: "Day Cycle"

South Dakota Review: "Addiction"

Stone Canoe Online: "Pilgrim Roads"

The Threepenny Review: "Remoter Margins"

Tinderbox Poetry Journal: "Instructions for Border-Crossing"

Valparaiso Poetry Review: "Zion"

Waccamaw: "Bethlehem, PA"

Yemassee: "Checkpoint"

"Optimist Club" was published in a broadside as the winner of Hotel
    Congress's 100th Anniversary Poetry Contest

I would also like to thank the following institutions for their generosity in
    providing support and residencies: Arizona Commission on the Arts,
    ART 342, Cornell University, Blue Mountain Center, Ora Lerman Trust,
    Petrified Forest National Park, Provincetown Community Compact,
    Risley Residential College, Sewanee Writers' Conference, and Truman
    Capote Writer's Fellowship.

Thank you to Lisa Sanditz for allowing me to use her gorgeous painting *Earthships and Their Neighbors* for the cover art. Likewise, I am grateful to the Herbert F. Johnson Museum of Art for permission to use the image.

I am grateful to my many teachers, mentors, and workshop leaders at Cornell University, especially Kenneth McClane, Alice Fulton, and the late Denis Johnson.

I am much indebted to Alfred Corn and Maurice Manning, as well.

There are too many friends and fellow writers who were instrumental to this collection to do justice in acknowledging here. Nonetheless, I want to single out a handful that helped to shepherd my work along, whether through comments, guidance, or inspiration: Jared H., Nick F., Ben G., Ezra F., Tacey A., Chris K., Meredith T., Abe B., Jamison C., Ted M., Cybele K., Fayçal F., Aeron K., Chris H., Phil M., Lawrence L., Andie F., Rob W., Les H., Megan C., and Josh C.

Lastly, a big thank you to David Mason for selecting this manuscript and to Alex Pepple for editing it.

Foreword

A MERICAN POETRY CAN be as discouraging as America itself—so many constituencies within their identifying ramparts, offering the rest of us little more than grievances. It can feel as if poets have entirely forsaken readers beyond a narrow circle of friends and colleagues. Few of our contemporaries imagine dining "With Landor and with Donne" or any other writers of the past. Few seem able, like Whitman, to imagine readers of the future. We are locked in the droning hive of the contemporary moment, busily "liking" each other, exalting self-affirmation over struggle and the difficult precision of art. And all the time we wonder whether it matters, when evidence of poetry mattering is out there, all around, in popular culture and politics as well as the classroom.

As a poetry reader, I am not seeking attitudes I can agree with. Poems are not opinion columns. I seek experience, a way of seeing into the life of things, a way of speaking that goes beyond formal competence to quicken my interest, slow me down and make me see.

Will Cordeiro's *Trap Street* won me not with its vision of America's desolating ephemera, at times inevitably reminiscent of film noir's stylized bleakness, but with its deliberateness, its verbal dexterity and modest authority. The poems feel lived as much as written, written as much as lived. Readers of this book may at times discern a too-unhappy fatalism trapping a failing nation, a too-steady gaze on dead and dying things, but I advise them to be patient and look again. This poet fully inhabits his landscapes. "Earth's everything I am," he writes, a declaration that can be read more than one way. He evokes this being and this planet vividly, and such evocation is itself a kind of love.

You can see this in the steady pentameters of his first poem, called "Open Country" as if the land were an open wound:

Then past some cloverleaf, a Motel 6
shines then dims, its ice machine still laughing
to itself. A vacant moon tricks out the clouds
over fields like gold we have no standards for,
far jack pines sopping up the last dark light.

That oxymoron, "dark light," could be a key to the book's entire mood.
Like Robert Frost, Will Cordeiro is a guide who only has at heart our
getting lost, but we can trust him, partly because he is lost along with
us, and partly because he pays attention, he knows the names of things,
and he does not avert his eyes. He knows what work is, what suffering is,
what death is, so the pleasure comes in how he knows and how he writes.
    A very different poem, "Route 66, Petrified Forest," pours out an
American scene in one unfinished sentence:

Ravens squawk on toppled outcrops
over each vista, guano the signboards,
tour guides to gaudy sediment, ledges,
cinder-tops; they scuffle and truckle
through snow-blind and -driven, wind
-eaten mud steppe, bad paradise that's
buckled to crumble of concrete, crucified
poles strung out by the highway, weigh
stations, casinos hemmed in by buffalo
chips, trap shops where they import dream
catchers, kachinas, geodes, and suckers
with tiny scorpions stuck in their centers:
billboards for jerky near sun-blistered off
-ramps railroaded as rawhide, past brush-
tips and char marks, ghosts of old road-
trips, carhop and heyday, this whole half
a continent dust-bowled—bulldozed aside . . .

The lines are deliberate in their cacophony, packed and jangly, making them hard to type as you try to remember how one sound follows another. A list poem, almost a found poem of western detritus, its jagged edges evoke an abrasive landscape—the way this nation turns its citizens to leather.

Cordeiro does not write only about the desert. He has lived in several different parts of the country, including its coasts, which he observes with the same careful detail. He knows the borders, the limits people find or place on their own lives. *Trap Street* is a map of vanishing dreams, true to the country as it struggles to exist. Yet the person who inhabits these poems has dignified the writing of them with real care and an ear for the elevated vernacular. His declaration that "Earth's everything I am" runs through every page of the book, mordant, restless, and abiding.

—David Mason

Contents

Trap Street

Clearing Ground

Wracklines

Badlands

Home Truths

A trap street is a fictitious entry in the form of a misrepresented street on a map, often outside the area the map nominally covers, for the purpose of "trapping" potential copyright violators of the map who, if caught, would be unable to explain the inclusion of the "trap street" on their map as innocent.

— *Wikipedia*

People are trapped in history and history is trapped in them.

— James Baldwin

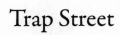

Trap Street

Clearing Ground

Open Country

You scan the foothills where an outline shifts:
each vaster distance gives a clearer view
within—each vista where you look and look,
and every figure is transformed to nothing
but shadows walking at the edge of dusk.

Then past some cloverleaf, a Motel 6
shines then dims, its ice machine still laughing
to itself. A vacant moon tricks out the clouds
over fields like gold we have no standards for,
far jack pines sopping up the last dark light.

Ride on. A scarecrow gnawed to sticks and rags;
a hide left curing next to guts it's spilled,
which tortured flies have claimed by squatters' rights.
One day your heart will rot like gopherwood.
You'll wake and watch a river pour away.

Landscape with Bureaucracy and Owl

The thimbleberry toggles
        in a breeze where forests were clear
-cut, raw foothills of stumps. I get up,
upload the blue

transmutation, predawn, fog's
        half-life elapsing, burnt drifts, grizzled
loggers lumbering to work; smoke
in the 5 a.m.

fauvist euphoria this side
        the valley. I'll remember if
rallied now, slowly, if seized, delivered
to downpouring

outbreaks of sun, how the rock-
        face and tree packs stood before
blasting. Wedged between these depressions,
the metagrobolized

town, a cobble of houses,
        begins lacing with cloud-light.
A barred owl out-rockets a ledge, swings
past the fire-

works depot, takes a mouse then
        cover in a defunct lamp socket
over a gravelly bed's steep run
-away truck ramp.

Skidders haul off split
        cut through back-
roads. Chokers lash old growth.
Scuttle cull; stack

up the cold deck. We put
        down the pike pole, the cant
hook. Daylight stalls, tax
forms and sawdust.

Cenotaph

In the translation you're reading
every word's wrong; faded pages

label the moon a pastiche. Say the sun's
made of cheese. Despite global warming,

the cows keep on farting. Silos rise up
like rockets, nearly bursting with grain.

The stars roll their eyes. Old rubbers
swim with an oil-blot's spectra, river

away, bright with poison & gnash.
The alveoli's dark matter might

collapse with each breath. Our future
is eyeshine from beasts on the margin.

At endtimes like tonight, any stray light
could walk through a door. Slowly, just

so. Oh, go gentle this time, sir. Moan me
a name. Hold me close to the pulse, blue

tremor of silk. The wind's unchaperoned.
Now, glimmer an instant. Move & forget

why you came. *What is salvation?* This
life—this life, it has never been yours.

Bethlehem, PA

Rain phosphoresces as the steelyards fade.
Each worker takes a drag. Exhales. Black clouds
turn bluish—surfaces hallucinate
in rivered sewage factories cough out.
Nothing happens here. Then less does. So on

and on, we become entangled in our beards
while picking holes through every shirt we own.
Men broken by the promise called careers.
He grabs his hunting vest, Sundays, and shadows
through bracts and deadfall for some venison

then stalks toward a bar-and-tackle, blotto:
one more shot—one more round to finish him—
below the same glum moosehead always smiling.
Men trade the dirty joke their fathers groaned.
Scrawled news loops by on boxcars, cursed for miles

past slag of foundries, burnt-out jags, and stones.
A bum lies frozen in the park. Who cares?
More roadkill bloats and festers on the shoulder.
The beer suds wink; the town's one long hard stare.
I've done nothing all my life save growing old.

Umbra Season

The wind can guide me but a little way
before the forest fans into an aimless
scuffle; each branch soon dips its neck, soon
tips to flicker in the breeze. I check
the trail, its marks redacted where new shoots
entrance the crumbled logs, where thorns exchange
scant dust that thickens over revanchist cairns
all gloomed along a backlit scrum of weeds.
These chancy tracks I'm brooding on keep forking
until they've canceled my expansive moods.
I straggled in these woods when I was young,
so thoughtless of its quick and ragged growth,
such paths that trick one into haggard tread.
Cicadas hum. Long days of summer—voice
a familiar's I am searching for. Past fern-thick
ruckus pilfering rubble, this jellied pulp
of greengold scum I shuffle through. The future:
a book that's locked inside an empty room
within a house I've only dreamt. I linger
past the space the ponderosas carve.
I limp on gravel that no maps can trace—
bloodrush of aspens through fine cinder heaps,
rootstock that ravels underground and loops
through dross so simple it would have no name.
Needlegrass frisks me on the narrow trail,
which feeds the mushroom's gelid fruiting. Quisling
decomposition. Nestling grubs and brackets;
splinters giving relish to the gribbles,

woodlice feasting under every relic,
spores peeking out. A brittle wilt remarks
the understory's decline. A hipbone strewn
near gnawed-off vertebrae bleached clean
divulges hunger and its many teeth.
If I were lost, I'd listen to my echo
folding back as if a prayerful call,
then circle round until I tracked my prints;
I'd use the iron in my blood for compass.
I'd seek a stream and follow its parade
then drink my aging image up. I'd let
the lightning touch the soft spot on my head,
that highest point where sodden days revolve.
I'd stray where mangled sedge gets trampled
right out toward an edge of living fire—
tall bunchgrass angled into shards of sun.
I'd scamper up a mountain nearing dusk
and pitch spare parts and gristle in a midden
which then I'd knap with flint until it sparked.
But I'm not lost because I've kept myself
composed, a steady cadence nudging me
along. I stroll toward the wild blossoms
spilled through marsh that fills the lower ground.
The wispy sludge sunfish pick primly over
along round moss-slicked stones sunk in the creek
could be the lap of that young girl who drowned
last winter. Lace of clover peeks through snowdrops
and frays what once had been her floral dress.
A silence now betrays the faceless center
of trunks and twigs, the deadfall scarred and damaged,
on the brink of tatters, charred. A silence

settles on the twilit briars, an eerie rapture.
Each mingled cloud lays down its shade in folds
as if a struggle had impressed the field
with shapes. Now I undress and span myself
into a pasture, yielding to be bedded
down as if I elbowed strangers—rangeland
stuffed with bones of buffaloes and arrowheads.
All through the small disaster of this afternoon,
I've fled a shadow snapping at my heels
and snagged on stalks until I fell.
I've come upon my life and want it back.
The chaff arrays in silhouettes, a canyon
bleeding out. All routes to home were long
ago forgotten. Every trail leads into dark.
But looking past all last year's rot, a compact
fritter from which rabbit brush and lupines,
forbs and coyote willow rise and dapple
with countless other tiny shoots and glumes
spackling the butte with seeds and flowers—I
half close my eyes, recline into a crush
of bristles, and assume my ease. I'm ushered
down each inch of the horizon's burn
like any piece of tinder. Wind goes by.
The beetles tickle as they braille my skin.
I sink into the weeds, a slow embrace
of grass. Daylight fails. Frail thistles glisten.
I laze away. Earth's everything I am.

Freight Journal

glacier mark, cloud-polyp—
breakdown
lanes & heartbroken lullabies through blood-borne
undercurrents: drop-
seed meadows,
                strata relics

a wind-combed sun gallops
past the talus ravel
& sallow luster of noise barriers
shower-stops &
lone erratics

*

we've been amber'd
in the umber evening

filterless & black lung'd,

twilit & twilitter: 10-4 & out

past Hackensack,
past Scranton

a scant wrack of self-splinter
through endless asphalt's blear hypnosis—

hollers rutted into mucoid cinders
gutted moonscapes hooked on fentanyl

*

faint venous-drip of autumn's serum

                    —a ruptured workaday
                        of wakened rapture—
a ghost-star
slipping
in a sinking river

each ferrous grain of slurry-fill,
fog & aura; scar & boulder

all smoldered in the far-out quarries.

Fractures

Not far off the farm, we stumble on
        truck tracks smack into frack-
ing: scumble and klieg lights. No

fence or barbed wire, bare zone
        of a work site, hilltop and dirt
bed, gravel and warnings—bag-

gage that towers the river. Lines
        of porta-potties under a big god
-forsaken rigged-out and gaudy

crane-looking thing. It's a landmark
        for miles, without moratoriums
here, pumping 24/7. Factions and

splinter groups, senators, PACs,
        each send out their peoples to snap-
shoot and leer, to test or to protest

drilling Marcellus shale. Hard-hatted,
        one gruff guy on his smoke break, tipping
his shades, gives us a stink-eye; hits

a last puff, then reflects on the rushes
        that tussle our direction, by gutters
where real estate swallows fat green

frogs, shallow glades, steep grades
　　　　of a meadow (lush choir of croaking);
hushed nondisclosure for those under-

signed. We've all seen this trick, you run
　　　　a spigot—figuring it's common tap
water, but in it a lit match goes ka-boom

and blooms into fire. Nights blazed
　　　　with a beacon; days, we've noticed
our cameras won't work in the bull-

dozed path of its shadow. No info leaks
　　　　out. You feed an unbroken horse baby's
breath and core of an apple. Later, turning

for home, out of roaming, down
　　　　dusty lanes "not approved for gas
co. use," by stables made over, trash

fires unwatched, a retrofit plowshare
　　　　landscaped as space-junk, men riding lawn-
mowers to bars, thunked mailboxes

chunky as lard cans, yards sunk under car
　　　　blocks, hole-fills, and rotor-tilled gardens;
past pipelines and privet, the last sign

on the block proclaims: "free manure."

Ephemerata

Walden Pond State Park

Late afternoon, we walk the pond's circumference
past the hot-dog cart
in the auxiliary parking lot on a path fenced in

to prevent erosion. I drown in one last drink while sunfall starts
its touch-and-go as if my heart's been fed
into a paper shredder.

Rucked in this fluvioglacial
sump, middle-aged swimmers in wetsuits slap and belly
over putty-water to reanimate their youth.

They hope for a good shiver. A tour guide points out the riddled erasures
on the rubble
while we read the decomposing litter-lumps: direct

mail letters, stumps of Styrofoam, wrinkled
cellophane, etc. Earbuds on a woman in a lotus-pose coach her

breathe in   *breathe out*

More careless shaking in my hands, and
sauntering on, the bitmap's blurred to chafed leaf-matter. The touch-
screen on your cellphone asks me if I want it saved.

Let the instant have it,
all this splendor. Each step,
a falling. The little cabin by the tracks is just an uninhabited

replica. Across the waters' reverie,
clouds sever and cohere: reckless scraps of neoplasm. Almost
November, shutter-lag decrypts the shadowed over-

cast and redder under-stitch
below those ragged white
flags of surrender.

Day Cycle

Morning—it's burning
in my thighs already,
and I climb a steep green crest
then let my burden
carry me on down its slope,
this summer when I'll have no rest.
Northern Colorado, somewhere
between Windsor and Loveland,
wind fractions and glimmers off
a lake that's used to
launch small pleasure
boats. This, my last full day
before I'll call somewhere else my home.
For now, I swerve past shrouds
of smoke floating from the foothills.
Piñons hug the boulders, canyons.
Miles fade through a slow unrolling
haze of folds. The mule deer flushed
into the lower culverts. Asphalt
falters, bakes, and blazes: a noon-lit
act of pure self-
                    variance: I ride
the shoulder on my shadowed blur.
I think how resin's melting
in the lodgepole cones, each twisted bolus
furthered by the smolder so that new ones
might arise. I reach a summit, blinking soot.
I gaze across a continent's divide,

a spine uplifted from this molten drift.
Small fires live inside all tinder—fallen
needles catching like a quick-strike book.
Going back, I bank a rim, sweat,
and glisten. I feel the bends careening
counter to me past vast dropseed meadows:
jimson, yarrow, fireweed. I fork
past hinterland that's buffaloed
with straw-toned buffelgrass. Summer,
long-suffering and raw. Faint
mountains flicker hugely golden
where darkness overtakes them.
I pump an incline, waiting for my heart
to give. Cruising now, the whole sky torques.
Beyond a crease, far cloudbanks
glow with cinder. Sun's vamoosed
the peaks yet silhouettes an egret.

Hay Bucking

That eighth-grade summer I was just a shade
above a buck sixteen, a would-be freshman
on the cross-country team who ran ten miles
afternoons, bone-tired, after mornings scuttled
from picking peppers on my hands and knees.
One day past midpoint of the break, thick clouds
gaumed up and billowed darkly in fraught portents
as I slogged into work. "It rained last night,"
Jake muttered, chewing on a blade of straw,
"and looks like rain a-coming. Best hitch in
the bundles fast before the downpour soon
or else the hay will mold and grow a fungus.
Could even burst in flames if waterlogged."
I nodded sure, not one to analyze
his terse and contradictory country logic,
and hoped for torrents, but of course was thankful
for any reprieve from the crawling hours
spent chucking ripe poblanos into buckets.
We took the truck and packed the bales in stacks
then levered up each sodden load toward
the next top-heaver under-slugging silage
until it dropped into the silo, snug.
While looking off to heaven if thunder shook,
I heaved up hay bales over half my weight,
those toppling burdens cradled and released.
With every catch and grip and swing and loft,
my brain was rattled and my muscles ached.
And then it mizzled and we had to toss

the hay bales quicker—snatch and pitch.
Each raindrop fatter as we hustled fodder,
those bricks of hay took off, off-kilter, flicked
no faster, farther than my crookback frame
could make them fly. At last, a laggard, I winged
one up which tumbled in a gap—as I
went teetering, fell backwards and capsized.
And all I know is next day I woke up
all-over broken, tender, oozy edges
in places like my toenails and my armpits,
as if I'd been raked over by an adze;
my shoulder blades like spastic skewers, tendons
racked in knotted folds, my sinews lactic
slurry. I couldn't drag myself from bed.
I lay there, aching. Eking out the minutes.
The bane of gruntwork made my flesh no more
than harrowed plots raked up by trundled needles.
Haggard, limp, I slumped in every sprawlful limb
like timber of old walls all fallen in,
a bonehouse sagging in its very marrow.
Called in that day—and didn't run a week—
and Jake worked harder, wrung with worry for
quiet burnings in the barn bowed flush with hay.

Pilgrim Roads

I.

Long days of hazed debris
on roads past cows and corn;
a blur all summer is,
parched land the sun has torn.

Towns disappear from maps
between worn folds. Folks die
to move but feel as trapped
as junked-blocked auto bodies.

The distances unravel,
miraged above decaying
highways that I've traveled
where eyesight's burned away.

I'm empty with no second
chance, no coming second act:
my crossroad's final reckoning,
a churchyard's cul-de-sac.

II.

Ditchwater spangles jewels
in antifreeze-green slop.
Tracks itch at every fool
to jump a passing hopper.

Spring mist, a Turin shroud.
Old six-pack rings, bindweed,
and flyers rain has fouled . . .
A turboprop recedes

beyond the edge of prayers.
I walk low-lying meadows,
a graveyard's disrepair:
heartland of rusted metal.

A nimbus covers barns
down corners lurching back.
Our seeded clouds now mourn;
the emptied streets contract.

At the Wheel

Stuck at a light next to a defunct church
sprayed *What the fuck is hydrofracking, bro?*
my engine overcooks. I hit the clutch.
I idle out. Smoke stretches from the hood,
a sketched-in shepherd's crook. The sun shellacks.
The kingdom of Heaven is within you, a pathogen
that syrups the blood. I fiddle with the radio
past static, country, crank-calling shock jocks,
call-in smack-talk, giggling porn stars,
past a susurrus of shucking corn, hard
rock that's crackling between a doomsday
pastor's foul gray moods, his sermon blasting
the born-again about those still unborn.
I haunt myself. The field I gaze at mocks me:
an empty fairground, a pockmarked weed-lot
rank with insecticides and auras. Each autumn,
the pink prize-pigs root through their slop, ear-tagged
and fattened for the market. Chops, loins, shank
and shoulder, spareribs, baby-back, porkbelly, hock,
and rinds; lard, orts, and gristle scrimped for scrapple.
The blinking gyroscopes go tottering. A Ferris wheel
locks up—a high school couple making out
on their private terrace above the scent of funnel cake.
A carny cackles, *Don't just cuddle. Put two fingers in her, boy.*
Nothing drops into the bucket-toss. Hot cow-plops
lampoon new suckers in a boondocks lotto . . .
The truck behind me blares. I look up for the sign.
Greenhorn, I tell myself, it's time to go.

I grip the key.

        My Civic sputters and I turn in traffic.
I hurry past the slurry fills and gutted strip mines' slather;
evade hillbilly cops who sip warmed-over sludge, clocking
radar—these Dogpatch speed traps, bully for the locals.
Over bedrock craters, rack, and asphalt rubble,
relics in my potholed brain burn off like fossils;
vision blackens with a belched exhaust.
Backfire below a fenced-in flatbed. Brown drowsy
faces creased with loam: pieceworkers jostled
by a buck and promised day of labor.
One lost man wanders in the breakdown lane,
his body twisted like a paper-clip,
a slipped hip listing from the miles he's withstood.
I turn for home—ungodly light,
dark wine and blood—
as evening drowns us all again.

Decay

Whole days spent looking out across the lake.
Cold mizzle glistens on slick beards of moss;
dizzy raindrops wriggle from a spider's thread.
Blue mountains levitate in far-off tones

of gray, and morning takes its slow time with
the burnt-off revenant of fog's decay.
Each waterbug is bent on its reflection.
Squirrels corkscrew up the paper birch,

my brain-roots dawdle into rotting humus.
One bloodshot loon seems evidence of folly:
my own, that is. A residue from last
night's bender. Blundering out the door,

I step through brackets of lush maidenhair
toward the dock. I strip and jackknife under,
scud and shiver off my melancholy,
then find a cadence heading for the point.

I drizzle as I lurch out from the water,
lie smitten in a play of patchwork sun
until the stupor that I'm in relents.
Perhaps the mushrooms lift their skirts. Perhaps

I could love whatever—earth moist and giving
below my feet—since no distinctions matter
when weather gunks up reason. These latter days,
the rings of each trunk fatten. Curlicues

of vines go tangling off into themselves
then reemerge as if a memory
of something golden twisted them that way.
I sit with languor now a little longer

and hear an earwig dig inside a burl.
Cloud-break spills cider over hazel grass.
First touch of autumn in the Adirondacks,
I think how all my thinking will become

groundcover flush with acorn caps. Shadows
maraud the copper scraps at dusk; birds rush
away like orphaned sparks of fire. Come,
I tell the darkness. Take your time. Erase me.

Daylight Savings

October's smoke-sweet drift sweeps off and floats
this crisp last day before the clocks wind back
while ear-small bones of light catch in the throat,
and sun motes shiver through each shifting crack

the tree-line's made. Soft hillsides bruise. Again
you'll go away wherever work—no, life
must take you. So, an hour gained is gone,
and we remain, just kicking stiff gold leaves

which riddle every step on stones we graze.
Slabs drizzle into gauze of sludge: a standstill
where any path might cross a hidden grave.
A buck with ivy tangled in its antlers

starts up then darts into the woods. The deer
bounds over broken scrollwork, wood-rot's glut
of moldered scurf. I squint—a day, a year—
and each impression pulses as I shut

my eyes. Then blink. Each ice-tipped blade is parsed,
starched grass that meadows all the flesh I've read
where mouthdark shadows heal up rigid scars.
As flowers turn to fodder for the weeds,

the weeds by further wastes become obscured
as graveyards perish into green preserves
where animals may wander blind, assured
no other presence ventures to disturb

the foot-worn passages their hungers trace.
A turning point—torn cloudbanks meld and baffle.
Snow simplifies the brake's bare ground. We gaze
one empty minute on these lives' spent gravel,

and wish to hold each other, but we walk
alone instead, to browse each mark and crux.
We crush stiff crusts of frost through snapped-off stalks,
the fractured sounds of which now freeze the buck.

I have neglected you for several weeks,
tight-lipped or blunt with knowing you'll soon leave
while I must stay here buried in my work.
The deer's eyes gentle, then shine undeceived.

Backlit, his head ignites, a ten-point blaze
as if a candelabra. And the wild
fields leap with snowfall, though my touch betrays
each crystal. No, we won't be reconciled.

Transience

A girl arrives to take my place
        this first of June.
   By noon, I'm out—the car jam-packed—
and part with my apartment all too soon.

A few days at a friend's, blank space
        to fill before
   I leave again for some small shack
to write in sand against the wrack of shore.

Make do with my small handful; read
        another's books;
   avoid the chocolate bar of soap
and topmost drawers, wondering which box

my underwear is in . . . The road
        spans on, more loops;
   each highway blurs like skipping rope,
and with each leap I take (lost years elapsed)

I'm ever off and other: daily,
        stunned by the sunder
   that I've become, a newcomer
who dallies over, under, into some-

one else's life. Past drumlin hills and valleys
        eclipsed of sun,
   I'll rally as a beachcomber,
and pick the flush tide-trash that flashes from

what I mistake for hermit shells
      but, closer, proves
   to be discarded tackle tangled
in the drift, scavenged by the squawking droves

of gulls. For now, I'm siren-spelled
      within a borrowed
  loft—buskers on the Commons jangle
a timeworn song up to my open window.

Wracklines

August, Rehoboth Beach

A day, a day again—
                              then summer disappears.
                    Twilit breakwater, dragged-back
            gut-tracks of Sunday's gruel clouds . . .

A drag queen's scarlet glitter
            feathers across the blue under-
                        skin of dusk's eyelid: mascara
                                    smudge, cantaloupe horizon.

                                        I want to write the difficult,
                                    the necessary song. Instead I take
                            a long slow walk along the shore.

            The boardwalk's garrulous
                        with garish billboards; tourists lick
                                    salt-dust off margarita glasses; kids slap
                        whack-a-moles, racked skee-balls skid—

if only I remembered everything,
            I could be purged of it. If only
                        I could dredge that old galleon's cargo up,
                                    and grind out all its wreckage in a wink.

            But none of us are starfish that grow whole again
                        from each lost limb.
                                        When the waves drag out,
                                                    my heels dig in.
Smooth bottleglass, brittle mussel
                        shells, tangled strands of kelp, and mangled lures:

                        a *materia poetica* spewed out at low tide,
this vacant speech of lucid flecks and flashpoints.

            Ghost crabs skitter sidewise over surf-skim . . .

            Our love finds something to be squandered on.

Mirage

Stalled clouds have orphaned shadows on the dunes.
The tide turns in, lifts salt breeze through your hair,
as fading sunlight fills an empty room.

You smell a storm approaching in the air.
A door abruptly opens on the sea,
a deepened blue of bay that's laced with sails.

There is no plot. No, only vagaries
of sky foreclosed on summer holidays,
moon's influence on borders it repeals . . .

Light clarifies the wreckage left by waves
while beach-grass necks and sways all afternoon.
How easily one's life is paraphrased.

Cavities and Conduits

The goings-on are ongoing in the face
of fluctuating waves and weather: here

tiny blobs of nonplussed jellies bobble.
Slurries slush down funneled burrows,
bubbling as sand fleas breathe between

sweeps and swells. A quahog peek-a-boos
then sticks a foot out of its mouth—its bi-

valve shell. An urchin cocks spare toggles;
a hawk glides over slog in gullies. Horseflies
maculate into a clot: viscera they've muckled

down to snot and lingerie. Stalking, this spider
crab won't raise an eye—sideways in waysides

through twitterpated skitter-skating, flushed out
from under-lips along latticework of sticky reeds
in tide-pool shallows. Beachsides teem and drool

with sticky organs. All mush and crush, moon-
strange ducts and honey-swilling mucus: glottis

spit-shined down the compact, blotched jigsaw-
fitting innards. I am an anemone whose anus is
the same as its fat lip—I gaze into my rigging's

lacquer, its spooj and sugar. I'm tickled pink.
My body, a tubeworm fermenting in bacteria;

I romp catawampus down lickspittle twisted
Mobius strips. One silver flinch of splintered
minnows, rash inchlings, quicken an instant,

crazing slender shadows through rich rushes.

Relics

Some crush-chinked beer cans and an orange peel
under the rusted truss bridge evidence
I'm not the only one who's ventured here.

A kid who hooked or maybe someone out
of work has trudged past fish heads, firecrackers,
and mothwings mummy-webbed between cattails,

then darted off the ditch path down the bluff
by hemlocks larded with Dixie cups. A crick bend
truck beds rattle over. Perhaps they hankered

to see their face flash by in wrinkled water.
Raccoon prints scrawled around cracked crawdad claws
tell another story of vandals. A sump of sedge

where noonlight winks, a lip purls over fetid
pools. Dragonflies gloss air then zip away.
My dog root-sniffs around and wanders off

through thatch-clumped thickets lank with swampy hair.
Strewn bones licked clean with one hoof sticking out:
a dead deer yeasting in a patch of ground.

Big skeeterhawks above the water-skaters
blanch then scatter. Fleet, golden, mortal,
this brutal looting of the self's own power

scuds through tang and fetor; is havened, fated,
a private waste of each lean day. And saving
nothing, striving still, one glance conjectures

a clot of busy gnats—dark local weather—
which sizzles sharply visible above
this restless mirror, but vanishes as soon

as clouds part, brisk, to avalanche their dazzle.
Light bleeds off rainbows from a gash of oil.
Drizzle blanches. Rash, roiled currents gush.

Mudminnows skim the rushes. Scum reaches
for my feet. Such roots, such ruts I'd disinherit.
Frogspawn bobbles across translucent floods.

A sediment of bones and buckled guts.
Beside me—beside myself—I now detect
small fanlike fossils on the slabs of shale.

Devonian clams or scallops. Slurry of
the muck I stand on slowly flows away
and hardens. Hollowed landmarks buried under-

water millennia ago. Now the gorge banks
gurgle, etched in with finials of trilobites
like secret figures in my cretin heart.

Rain lashes down. The river heaves. It claims
these small impressions . . . I'll let others puzzle
the shifty smattering my pad-marks leave.

Provinceland

Our address: one sun-parched, purple starfish
that's nailed up by the steps, past tiny toads
who sponge rust-colored water from the well.
Carom the ridgeline's dusty road, slantwise,
then curl inward, earward as a sea-snail's shell
to our front porch. Here, trash dangles overhead
like thought-balloons, to keep it from the mouse.
Daylong, waves slap and hiss beyond the crest;
hawks tilt the thermals; vireos and warblers
veer back then scissor out the caramel dunes.
Our clapboard's tucked in next to spiders' nests
that lace the huckleberry. A craze of pollywogs
in muck-tracks squiggle up, iotas, near
squiff understories of earth-stars, lady's slippers,
a mermaid's purse that's dropped close to the house.
Gray seals gulp air then dip down swift trapdoors.
A fluke of breaching humpbacks breaks the summer
haze, like tears set loose in hazards of the sun,
which fall into the ocean's sizzled shards—
the clear-eyed promises of afternoon
have bleared the plural of all blues as each
bleached stone's true color shines in surf. One red
kite jukes above the slope.
                          We search the beach:
warped cargo, sculls, and cork-pocked rubble belched
on brittle driftwood wobbled up the littoral.
From pinchbeck scumble we have made ourselves
small trinkets, which we pitch back in the shelf.
Mosquitos thrum the blood-decaying light.
The bilge and wrinkled spume—shell, sluff, and spill
of jellyfish, of sea scum give us pause.
We shuffle home before the sundown's done.

Fluencies

Light steps over
riverstones. A scrap of cellophane,

its spectra leap,
efflux roils

in yellow flame. Clouds empurple; eddies purl—
a fish glints by.
Sun flashes foil.
Bottlecaps   pop
tabs   abandoned tires   etc.   A current
drags its slurry
on.   Its bubbles scumble   wobble   wink:

more crimpled
junk   more random
rubble
sliding forward.
Black garbage-bags

& High Life empties,
formless slag &
plastic forks—

Stray bits of skin no one can salvage: hard scar tissue, frayed dreamwork & a baker's yeast of theory-parts

—this quick still point my ankles wade in,
blank river'd days all going past it, cascading seizures,

leached-out gravel   the on-going rankled in its late descent.

An hour standing here
in shallows
doing nothing   hurriedly.
My inner descant
discontent.
Hour waking
slowly   slowly
fated   darker   only blink:
leave-taking hour
flowing flowing—
no shard is saved, no truce but what is sieving through me.

This lucid hour,
useless   faded   spent.

Dune Maze

Past slash of beach grass cross-
winds spin in halos, this sift of

trailheads loping over shoulders
berserk in ersatz ziggurats. Lop

-sided cliffs jigsaw a bluff; re-
shuffle clefts with coleslawed

muck where stippled bird-tracks
hieroglyph. Ripples shift. Over-

grazed, slopes scarp across a haze
of sinkholes, blunted by the dwarf

pine. Tides ruck bleached-out drift-
wood, spindrift, pinkish beach-rose:

mosquito beds in marsh march up
the brackish backwaters & stubble

scrub moss with heron nests as
nettle masses flick a threadbare

glare across the fastness. A snatch
of shell this far inland is seized &

snuffed to scurries of debris: any
ruffle in the benthic zones would

bubble up a sphagnum bog
or boggle over kettle ponds.

The cloudroads perish overhead
as plovers brace against a breeze.

Each seizure-trace is torqued into
a self-effacing loft of serried herds

as tourists probe against the grain
then race a loping scurf, an addled

edge they're adding to: all carried
away by the current's errant urge.

Eroded Shell

O
cold
water,
where its
hiss
is locked
& it turns through
the ear's own mazing,
each
gap hips out &
lathers light between a broken loop
inside this lapidary
jewel-box . . .
The sea itself entangles in
sheer grizzled hair that petrifies: look at this pink
ribboning that braids away into its dark-most touchfire carapace,
now abraded till it's nearly lace,
loose iridescent spell.
& woven here we see
the dream-shaped waves swell up, sink, somersault—spill
over, sough & sail away . . .

The mind's pure spire
within the body's labyrinth. A star-spent frieze
of froth disperses into traceries, all spume
& lineaments of form,
more water
rushes—reaching in
toward the bone to fill each brain-
fold's
lip with a frivoled slush
of nacre,
a lacework's
pulp—marrow, sap,
scum,
shellac;
a blind thrust
of vectors
trumpet,
near a
zero-
ing
in
.

Herring Cove

Tonight the moon's bewitched the paths
     of sails that trail no wake
   while dream-slow slime's the better half
of snail-feet dipped in tide-pool baths.

Incessant wrack throws broken tons
     onto the fleeting sands,
   which shift down dunes and scrape undone,
caressing dreck they're drifting from.

That boat out prowling on the bay
     deludes the flagging eye
   with cheated curves of lunar rays
stretched out in cloud-borne shadowplay.

The chill winds howl like children lost.
     Spray rakes the naked rocks
   where slurs and hooks stir over gloss.
Each lobster pot's half cracked or tossed

lopsided by the tides. Fishwives
     stitch seine-nets up with knots.
   Eels glide and tangle through their weaves
while dropping shelves cause swelling waves

to smash each shell to shining ooze
     within dark veils of kelp.
   The bottom-feeders form a bruise
where ghost crabs skitter; plovers cruise.

A foghorn beckons through fine mist.
A seal snouts up for air.
Perplexed small craft here can't resist
old whaler hulks that blot what is

this margin of lost, junked routines.
The lighthouse shines,
then sweeps away—its beacon gleaming
over liquorish foam and bones picked clean.

Aubade, Provincetown

Up, cold crux and fold, at morning's crack,
sun crests the freckled shoulders of the dunes;
sand-quick, each hour hustles off the spume
that blooms and dies as soon as it is born.
My eye's the skeptic that the sun has torched.
Gray clapboards fade. The mind sees through the sky

across its tiers of sherbet from the porch.
All day, the waves wave blue, wave blue goodbye.
By noon, each shadow-over gets absorbed,
high prop planes humming like scaled dragonflies.
Slopped rockweed slathers on the shore's slick bed;
a riptide's gash is left unsatisfied.

Old anglers leave spilled guts, stripped fishbones scattered,
which lure out crowds of gulls to cruise and pick them.
Fat wood-bees Jacob up their unseen ladders.
The beach keeps wiping off its makeup. Look—
I spot a distant spout, one far-out fluke.
A blowhole spurts. The waves keep turning tricks.

Evening

Warped dunes indent
                    before they smudge
          & then eclipse into the dwarf
      pine. Unchaperoned,
the clouds' flamed
                underbellies prowl.

            For hours now
                            I've failed to paint the sea's faint edge,
      its wash of sun-bled residue. Clockwise above,
                        the terns are killing it.   I mean, they're killing

time. A nimbus brushes every tip
                        as valleys slant away. Beach grass
        italicizes.   I swish my muddled
                            glass.   I come to terms
          with blue & umber, cobalt, gesso,
                    dioxazine, viridian & every varied hue

                        of mauve within the movement of each
                            cruel wave—
                                        the ne plus ultra of ultra-
                                    marine
        that's ravishing this shore's
                    gray monochrome.
                                        More sludge
                                        crests up.
                        Spume & wrack;
                            flume & foam.

        Each sud has bleared the nearer distance.   Over-

            cast dayglow.
                        &
                    yes, all summer's wasted.   I am, too.

    The deerflies taste my blood.
                        A year, skipped
                            stones, sky's blush—hell, nothing
        changes, night coming on at last.

            One corner still remaining, a spit
                        of canvas that I'll stain & lavish.

        Small light I've made my own.

Fairy Tale

I took the ditch path back the empty lot
across the graveled patch of
scutch-grass, musk
thistle, the fox squirrel
.22ed and rotting,
coyote scat pebbled with undigested pustules

of huckleberries. Pollen-scattered air.
Busted beer bottles, lottery scratch-
off tickets, chickenbones—
alone, I followed
my ear:
thought of you then got over it. Stripped gristle

and leftover dressings of a deer. I mooned
around the clearing beside the quick-
spilling wash. Not
everything must
have some cosmic meaning.
Cottonwoods mottled the breeze with wishing

stars, great clouded tufts. A salamander,
amphibian once thought shape-
shifting fire, slewed
through the water's
oily sluff and dander.
Far cliffsides red with iron like my blood.

Kept trying to make more of it. A fact:
the high weeds trembled
while my body, limp,
remembered sleeping
next to you. The fiction:
I could walk off. That any ending's simple.

Spiral Jetty

i.

                    against
        a gray & formless sky

                    longing to be raptured

            we drive for hours past capsized boulders
    strewn in empty fields:

                    wheatgold phragmite unraveling without one buffalo—

                        a patch of spike-rush   of pickleweed
            industrial gravel-pits
                        the Promontory Mountains in the distance
                past a center-point where the iron tracks
                                        of East met West—
                            some faint, mephitic rot
            from seagulls de
                        -composing
                                on the shore . . .

    & then a frail declivity:

                    we step out of the car
            across the vertex of the lava rocks

                                    each pockmarked where the lake's
                        been shriveled
                                    back by drought, looming cold & far—

ii.

                                            the jetty just a heap of stones—
                    salt-encrusted
                        keepsakes of basalt;

                the shallow lake still half a mile out:
                                    sucked back & lost—

                                        though its curve holds steady
                    like another turn
                                    / yearning to be/
                                        //nature //

            a gallery of lockstep stopgaps & aftershocks

                        forsaken
                            &

                        defiled

iii.

                                                    a wind now lures the water's
light
        slight variations
                    riven—
                        the current torn,

                                            unsettled;
            as if illusion
                                        were scoured & given form
                        upon the flats

iv.

                                                    delivered to the optic
                                    edge
                /where wind has parceled out

                                            its paradox/
        vast bed of salt
                    like snow, a barren parallax

                                    alien
                                    of anything that grows

                    we step into the dis-
            embodied,
                        on the counterclock
            -wise stones
                        & down
                            into a rock-ribbed time that

                                    time's forgotten—

v.

                                            a mass of windblown
                                foam
            jellies up into a hoard,
                                shivers,
                                        fribbled, jury-rigged &
        spastic—
                        some fraught thing
                which has no sympathy

                                        for us

Badlands

Route 66, Petrified Forest

Ravens squawk on toppled outcrops
over each vista, guano the signboards,
tour guides to gaudy sediment, ledges,
cinder-tops; they scuffle and truckle
through snow-blind and -driven, wind
-eaten mud steppe, bad paradise that's
buckled to crumble of concrete, crucifixed
poles strung out by the highway, weigh
stations, casinos hemmed in by buffalo
chips, trap shops where they import dream
catchers, kachinas, geodes, and suckers
with tiny scorpions stuck in their centers:
billboards for jerky near sun-blistered off
-ramps railroaded as rawhide, past brush-
tips and char marks, ghosts of old road-
trips, carhop and heyday, this whole half
a continent dust-bowled—bulldozed aside
where timber's been blitzed into flaws of
fossilized crystal: moonscape that's chiseled,
whiplashed, wiped clean, with ratcheting
lizards doing push-ups on stucco, fissile
matter whittled down to a clay we're made
from, eighty-sixed neverland, last strong-
hold for this herd of pronghorn which
unrivers and stiffens, nibbling the saltbush
at the edge of a yellowcake divot, a hushed
panorama scraped from sunbake and thorns.

Nizohni Point

Boneyards beyond each shadowed level,
blue sediment and nuances of far continua:

carved buttes and saddled clefts upshift and settle
while scoria accrues. A silhouette of kestrels cruises

over parched defiles; fields now darted, reveled,
flushed of rich brown nameless birds, which lob

and swing like lassos before each wing collapses
into flock, down thrust of rock that ravage lapses

200 million years, more or less, grafted-in and cobbled
to an unconformity of ash, some crusted trash the wind's

lobotomized. A wine-lit dusk—not much consolation
as the tiny spiders hobble on their remaining crutches.

Death of a Code Talker

Crammed in a doorjamb as part of the public
where a draft sweeps by, I'm shiftless in standing
room only, behind stiff marines, hushed hosts

of *Diné*, blond teens buzz-cut and dressed up
with pressed beige fatigues who keep shuffling
in more foldout chairs to seat the over-

flow of neighbors and elders, a storied
tribe assembled here for Keith
Little—big man, rancher, chief voice

for code talkers whose unbroken crypt-
ography once converted their language
into a weapon. Underage, Keith enlisted

by goading any friend handy to lend
him a thumbprint. "Now what
was that for?" the man who gave it

pressed him. "We're going off to war."
The man's skin already inked: *I should've given
you the finger*, I imagine his comeback

since the gravelly eulogist switches to
Navajo. Half the congregation laughs.
This is a speech which may well stand

at the threshold of extinction in a lifetime
or so. Uniformed in bolo ties, these soldiers,
now older and fragile, helped raise the flag

at Iwo Jima and saved the whole Pacific
theater. The services done, I'm driving over
barren ground, thinking of my abandoned

family; my ancestors who wrested this land,
this country which has never *not* been at war
with its people. As for the tours and the rest,

I've many misgivings about any nativist
bluster of American strength. Why
are raptured young soldiers transported

into battle with only a bystander's
notion of their histories—but pride
for a nation that's never loved

anyone back? A flag stuck at half-mast
snaps in a storm blowing up. My truck
passes a face concealed below a shadow

of Stetson, held fast against the traffic,
trying to hitch, his thumb offered out
to switches of dust—chaffing—quickly

lost, a ghost-owl crossed by a gust, translated
to wind . . . And maybe you'd be right
if you'd ask what part I've played in all of this.

Remoter Margins

In no-bit Western towns like Santa Claus
or Dead Horse Gorge, you've given up
on love, the past—its flash and patches—
coming back or not, the sentiments
you can't believe have given up on you.
Folks gawp at tin-roof shacks and dull brown yards
with broken slabs while yokels on their porches
dawdle empty talk. They rock and pap. For days
the only human contact you have made,
you couldn't bring yourself to say one word;
just nod, the waitress topping off your cup
until the coffee pot ran out. You pocketed
a couple packets of the cream then stole
one glance behind you as the door slapped shut,
your brain as ripe as yesterday's motel room—
road unthreading from the next plateau.
A traffic of slack years elapses. Let it.
Now clouds refuse to budge above the canyon.
You take your rucksack and a credit card,
its numbers worn so you can pick a lock,
and stink with beer while big rigs rumble by.
Strip mines and boulders cave in, slowly. A raven
circles in the bleached-out sky. Sit and think
here on the shoulder, about the pig you've been.
Your novel bludgeoned longer, crowded, wrong,
though not one page is written down. Hot wind
blinks gravel-dust along gaunt jagged plains
a river once ran through. Fate holds its grudges.

Presume to see clear to some water's edge
what's only heat above a strip of tar.
Another truck has passed you, and this is
the story you wake to and must live again,
one pissant town like any other since
your luck won't change. A beat-up Prelude stops
to ask where you are going. You say, the same
place you are, man. Just further down that road.

Optimist Club

Hotel Congress, Tucson

A boy sashays across the dancefloor's glimmers.
You catch his eye, one mascara'd glance, before
he's stolen by the baffled liminal menagerie
of lights. With each wheeled flash and shroud,
a crowd of bodies blends with lasers—veiled,
revealed in garlands centaurs prance among
as quasars fractal. Sandmen befuddled by the fog
machine and vampires scanty in the looking
glasses. Banshees wailing while you ogle outfits;
quick strobes decenter every solid fact.
A slender moment freezes. A slope of shoulders,
spaghetti tops, like slipshod snapshots blazoned
in hipshot poses by flip paparazzi . . .
Light skips again then stops. The brazen dark
has rollicked up a myth of razed empires:
all Rome, all London burning down, and Paris,
then you remember that this hotel once
blazed, 1934, the night clerk ringing
the exchange box; Humason could only save
his violin; guests screaming past the toppled
furniture, the engines gone berserk down 4th,
a single slipper lingered on the steps—
bleak gleams of smoke and murk as the police
filed in. They pulled one drunken sot from bed,
who sneered, "Shit, let the fucking place get polished
off in flames, I got my room paid up this week!"

All guests vacated, Dillinger included,
whose two stool pigeons asked a firefighter
to retrieve their duffels stashed with pistols, rifles,
more ammo than the cops possessed: a fool
decision since—a tip-off later—they've been seized
in handcuffs with the gang. Cool hundred grand
in damages. Burnt-out, rundown, the hotel,
like the country, sunk in a Depression.
Charbroiled dustbowls, junkyards, breadlines, and
train-hopping hobos scrawling secret signs
between the thresholds where handouts were had
or liquor could be swapped for work, if work
were not some Shangri-La.

                        So, jump-cut to
the mahogany bar with reconstructed trifold
mirrors. You order Glenfiddich on the rocks.
You people-watch this spun kaleidoscope
where every turn dissolves, fades in, and sparks
a fire from which they recreate themselves
as if *decadence could be an end in itself*—
but still this reckless stupor's just a truism
by which you cope with the colossal night.
You stare. An ice-cube's splintered with a star.
Its infant fame grows watery and soon
the blurry room seems like your tumbler's resin.
You butt-dial back a drunk-text sent, an ex
cathedra from your seat of learning; scroll
for late-breaking updates with your dwindling data,
swipe left, left, right—stock photos, selfies,
dick pics, flames, etc. Hope's sprung eternal, though

time's a zoetrope where motion is illusory.
The clock-hands folding into mocking prayer,
the pumpkin hour when wishes to the fairy
gods are hyped-up typos trapped in Bartleby's
dead letter drawer.

                    Downcast yet eager, high
despite this lowdown, you stroll to Tiger's
Tap Room, cast a side-eyed glance around,
awake to chance; your pit-stains ripening,
the music loud enough it shakes your flesh.
Your face half harlequin, half pixelated,
a serape of shadow where your image maps.
Erased. Your bloodshot cellphone gone to shit,
you now forsake the chase, tap out, and grab
a squat Red Stripe. You chug the sweating bottle,
say hello to friends. Mug a smile, mellow out.
A pessimism of intelligence, an optimist of will—
you wander second-guessing through the space
again until the DJ, scratching, cross-
fades and blends the rhythm of two tracks
into a catchy riff's hip-hop cadenza
which revs, then shifts, sped to freefall over-
drive, everyone jumping, hearts lifting when
the beat's been dropped. A wedding party
romping and improper now bursts out
breakdancing from the Copper Room, moist tuxes
crashing in. The joint is one incessant crush
like suppurating, dripping hexagons
cleft open from a honeycomb. This thrumming
buzz is actually your skull. The thumping bass,

your own lush pulse. Subwoofers raise the roof,
trepan the soft interior vibrations
imprisoned in your cerebellum.

                                    You step outside
onto the patio. Drink in the cooler summer air
beside the Cup where people congregate
to smoke. A hummingbird dips down and sips
a blossom over-spilling from a hanging
planter. Still, the club shuts down within the hour.
You study the cobbled walk you'll have to scuff.
Some stranger begs a light. You shake your head,
and yet he nods and flirts, "Hey, what's your name?
I saw you earlier." Then looking up, you see
that all your obdurate and daring anguish
had been projected. Confess one longing look's
possessed you, though you don't know anything
about him, by replying with a curt coy pout—
the rococo furnishings of eros that arose
from memory, that molten forge, when pressed,
unfurls one gorgeous glass-blown bauble of
a chandelier, its shape held fast, its surface changing,
as it prisms hard-edged facts so they give way
to plasma, a chasm bridged by ever-later styles
of fire, which burn all grief that came before.
You offer him a cigarette and graze his hand,
then take it; inching closer to this boy,
slack-jawed and skinny, making out—
that little bud of flame a voided rose.
The ash sifts off. Last call. A whiff of smoke.
You peek into the door, the chairs upturned,
as streetlights jackpot every tiled penny.

Manifest Destiny

Old Route 66

Long walk past sun-cracked faults
of country, trap rock trace
on highway given way
to riprapped, driven tor—

a roadbed's bedrock, vaults
of rusted flasks: rest place
scorched to flake, annulled. Pay-
dirt paved over, laved & scored

by sand-grains poured down
-wind. Come see America end
to end: hardscrabble towns
graveled, bellied up, or burnt.

By badlands past renown
this buffaloed, hell-bent
stained off-road trail of stones
tears off to no return.

Zion

A desert where the senses fail,
where everything's a relic—
we take the East Rim trail
past cottonwood and beavertail,
the scrub oak touched with yellow.

We hike the ancient seabed floor,
the limestone grooved, hipshot, and torqued,
up the ridgeline's crenellations,
a cliffside braced by juniper,
to keep our pace toward Weeping Rock.

Small lizards lightning underfoot;
the meridian dissolves our blood.
Wind trips the aspen's shivered light,
each leaf's wet premise of a star.
October: summer's over now for good.

The path remiss, a gallery of sediment,
we gully through a saddleback:
dead code of tracks
fans through the sage and meadowgrass.
A bighorn nimble on a crack

stares down a sheer crevasse.
Below, we bask
and twinkle in fall's lucid dust.
A basin holds us fast
while clouds ride shadows which envelop us.

Around a bend, the canyon drops
degrees of blue in air forever
until the trees look flat and level;
sun strikes the twisting river blind—
and down and down all's revelation.

Mormon Lake, Fourth of July

A year as lost as any paycheck's been,
and we've returned. This sour backwoods dive—
longnecks and empties scattered round the place,
a Saturday we've left the town behind
for any beer on tap, sawdust and sap of pine
—is all our own. A raucous boondocks where
Zane Grey, who hated Mormons, wrote *Riders
of the Purple Sage* while sitting at this table,
gazing at the formless lake. A small museum
displays his trophy game and paraphernalia,
photos of his record yellowtail and sailfish,
his Remington.
                    A saddle decorated
with swastikas, which causes a debate
about appropriation from the Navajo; his chaps
emblazoned in the stars and stripes. Cattle
prods, barbwire. Downstairs, a paunchy rabble
has been tipping back their scotch since noon.
Each musty room's been filled with buffalo
and pumas, foxes, elk, and antelope:
a shock of silk electric on their skins,
their glassy eyes a proud, a shamed inheritance.

We chug and squabble, leaning back against
snug Ponderosa walls each brand-marked black.
Cluttered, eclectic curios box in
a motley herd of farmhands, thickset wives,
small-time ranchers, ropers, anyone who's braved
the drive to wobble on a stool and say hello.

The house band plays familiar covers, Steve Earle
and Patty Loveless; the fiddler takes a break
to crack the spoons, and when every other
girl is shimmying on the dance-hall floor,
fast daylight leaving grain by grain, this earth
feels welcome late and soon.
                                        Feels good enough
that beer is cold, a dollar coin still warm
from where the barmaid held it in her palm.
Although the moon is young, we're all so old,
so middle-aged and tired of our lives;
these workaday routines which keep us poor
have kept us pleading one slow extra song
before going home from so much honky-tonk.
We're pining to concede some last excuse
to celebrate our past with ripped-off country.
We stagger with our lagers as we join
the masses gathered near the water's edge:
near deer-licks, sedge and cattail, listen to
the buffleheads and mallards squawking,
taking wing from off the lake and over
breathtaking miles of wild acreage. We cup
our hands and, puckering, exhale with lips
pressed tight; we do our best to make a gruff
call back, at first just whisper-like, decrepit
imitations—face our limits, a small flock
no more than shadows coasting through the dark
beyond earshot and soon forgotten echoes.

The town has said no fireworks this year.
The lake has shriveled into hollyhock
and tickseed, the air so dry such brittle

scrub's just waiting to catch spark. Yet volunteers
have sent up homegrown flares and willow rockets,
a few of which explode, a few which fizzle,
while Black Cats pop and spinners wheeze across
pea-gravel parking lots. A single whistle
travels up to flower. And for one moment
two great breasts of flame appear. It rains
pure ash and broken glitter. Smoke drifts off,
and then the same cold restless stars shine lost
through boundless space. Why any of it matters,
nobody asks.
                Hot bygone day's
again one long collapse, and slowly and
no wiser for it, come what may, we know
we'll die some quiet ordinary hour.

Fire Season

Down altitudes of chaparral and scrub,
a few green cottonwoods pronounce the valley.
High clouds their own detritus, lucid hour

when a panorama laminates itself
in memory, inviting the vagaries
we live by. Wind-twisted juniper

through listing fields. You search the vapored edge
while driving home—a place you can't escape.
The sunlight fans past lurching buffelgrass,

a single hunger not a city's hundred,
past dam-parched tableland and bluffs. Today
the fire danger is severe. A plume

rewrites the ground's unmappable terrain.
The heat denudes caliche and lavishes
a sweeping sheen as if the earth had gorged

on nectar, arranging dunes by increments.
Smoke glooms the glowing sunset lavender;
you follow light through grainy travertine,

a wish to look at things not through them
despite vast distances you navigate.
You squint ahead. A range where chaff ignites.

Arroyo

When shadows fall across the rimrock's face
from clouds set drifting in their lucid dreams
as if all knowledge tried to flee itself,

far mountains tremble in the predawn haze;
stray sand grains twist up tall as any man,
and each saguaro fades in silhouette.

The thorns—like proxies of torn, withered flowers—
hide nimble lizards skittering the cliffs
where fragments scatter over light-parched land.

Gold sifts to distant blue and raw pink luster
as hawks revolve below the scud and stratus,
above old scars of rivers flooding dust.

We live within the folds of rimpled maps,
forsaken days of increments . . . Come, hold
this globe. Its shaken remnants drift and glow,

this skull of something where the ants retreat
into a socket; bowl coyotes limp
to, mornings, slaking up a gathered dew.

Vistas

I.

An overlook of sutures, maars,
& eskers are a crooked rookery of
kestrels—continental loss, false
stasis of wind-wrestled buttes,
mute boulders, lewd solitudes;
the restless flood-carved wastes
that weathering & sun erase
are roughshod into this: damaged
country moonlight's plagiarized,
all boneyard, bluff & cold mirage.

II.

Another sundown's run
past rim & fastness, wind
quickening the grassland
above crossbeds & crusts.

A lone mule deer stands
twitching ears & canters
up the ridgeline's switch-
back until it's lost among

crags & scrub. Cloudbanks,
snowblink. Dune drift. I am
arrested by how swift light
folds like any wrist & locks

day down a canyon. Grama
swivels. Beyond an overlook,
a skewbald herd leaps off—
it shatters up a rattled flock,

black inverse of a blizzard.

Instructions for Border-Crossing

If tú taste the laced trickle of mineral, don't swallow
your spit. A broke-down tour bus can correr on bootleg rum
and donkey piss. Mejor to never complain that it's hot,
porque este lugar es justo tanta arena errante.
Otherwise, it's only seguro to talk about el tiempo. Sol y
more sun. Moral: no matter where you are, it's a gallery
of masks; enough enemigos in every espejo. Keep moving.
Pronto te alejarás. Don't ask—you should always run
down a list of alibis y piensa dos veces. Recuerda, English
is a type of spin. The skin-marks left by zip-cuffs leave
mapas viejos que están sangrando; rough terrain where leyendas
smudge into a sprawl of gaps, best sigues tu sudor donde gotea.
Chava, don't reason with coyotes, they'll write you off
as entre los que perdí. How many sisters hicieron desaparecer
in a haze across this slurry y basurero quemado, their trek
now a breeze through a maze of barrancas? Cuidado
de lava rocks y razor wire, the crosshairs of any Minuteman:
la luz de mediodía es un blister. Que solamente una cosa verde
could make this desert bloom. Cualquier papel te dan
means you have no say since each piece of ground's surrounded
by some barbs. Por lo tanto, hide your dinero en los snakeholes—
slide each trinket in a sink, burn every link back, and void your fake
windbreaker. Viaja en la noche but don't trust ningunas estrellas:
pueden caer. Grind your bootsoles on your one cuchillo bueno
until they leave no tracks. And if you're asked, just say you've nunca
tuviste un hogar porque the polvosa spot where you were born
has blown away. Avoid the pump-jacks' seesaws, blades of windfarms.
West Texas is a no-man's-land and el nombre de todos los ríos es mirage.

Encuentras algún trabajo, pero no estás aquí. So, if you're ever
startled at a stopgap spot check by la migra, patrol cars where buzz-
cut guardias wave you out and trip you up in small talk, determined
to make you fall behind, tarde al tu trabajo—their stiff German
Shepherd, trained to maul you, sniffing your pant-legs for whether
you've the whiff of mules—then hand your pinched card over.
He'll look you up, inch by inch, and down. Once, twice, he'll squint
at your foto, faded white as any leper. He'll scan it. Buen weather,
he might remark. Sí. Mira, días alegres sin fin. Go ahead, feel free
to point out you're not from around these parts. But really, hell
if it ain't a beautiful country. He'll have to agree. Una tierra de hierro
y un cielo herido ambos derramaron su sangre a través de una frontera.
Tell him that. See where it'll get you. Or rather, tell him some things
should just be kept separate—tales como oil y vida, agua and money.

Hawk Song

A hawk scythes
flaws of counter-
light over nettle
& beveled fields
of devil's claws.

Sun tightens like a screw into my head.
Feathers, stiffened over thermals,
coil. A lazy parasail above rimrock.
Sandstone fades to coral as haze
dims outcrops into further levels.

Past palo verde down a parched arroyo,
a river's phantomed—powder, gravel.
Nothing to survey. No hope for any dead
reckoning. Saguaros crucify the far
horizon. Dunes calcified & arched.

Heat waves strain eyesight to swoon,
dissolving each berm to boom
-eranging flames illusioning to gloss.
Memories evaporate. One whip-
tail skittles off, throat-pulsed. Stains

glimmering, boulders mass & shoulder;
mesas vanish into shadowed ochre,
shuddering another ridge: dust
devils sketch across an older knoll,
a mealy monument where wind's

scaled off the softest crust & cold
cracks up slack bluffs. Buff
canyons, talus crubble, top
-heavy benches settle. Subducted
uplifts eroding, crosscut. Over-

head, wheeling—wheeling—
a red-tailed hawk stalks
shade across the face
of earth.
         Its eyes hold fire
serrating every raided edge.

I have no feelings left.

Checkpoint

No going back. You pinch yourself, and if
you're there, then swallow down the twisted worm

that silks your thoughts. We've all been burnt, no warnings
what the factories belch; we've hacked black soot in shifts

of wind. We stitch the labels as they choose,
the boardroom suits, then fix what's porous;

how stiff, how overtaxed maquiladoras'
joints—they sell our passage for a truce,

tracers over razor wire. Floodlights switch
interrogation bulbs. Cross-pollination

over walls where every seed's been rationed.
One city gridlocked; one lost in its own grit.

More buzzards cauldron air. Gulls, back and forth,
swoop in to rag-pick off the dumping grounds.

They squabble with each other, choking down
their crumbs then head for Big Macs somewhere North.

El Niño quickens but the seasons slow . . .
Corn spliced in labs seduces parasites:

each kernel an impacted tooth. What might
be stoned where semis pass, where toxins flow,

and runoffs leach? Our desert's coming to
a boiling point. The rivers disappear.

Whatever marks the line is just as clear
(where trees hang lace from girls coyotes used)

as any boozehound's speech. It sounds like drones
when locusts wake: this land without one house.

Cross over now—step on your father's cross-
road. Sun's crossfire. A bridge of others' bones.

Homeward under Falling Stars

Sundown—we're driving over cliff-
& scrubland rife with twisted arms
of sprawled saguaros, prickly Shivas

that beseech to a long horizon kivas once
reached to, splayed upshifts & canyon rifts
& amber cuestas where spruce beetle kill

still riddles ground; weeds razor-wire over arid
wastes & cindered limbs. The rockslides splint
on scraggy hillsides, as we race round wayward

bends: trampled mountains, middens, stubble,
which erase to rubble riven down by missing
rivers. Evening's onslaught's as translucent as

the drapery of caves: a late, boneset blanch
of moon looms numinous upon the snow.
Ice blazes at this altitude amid the standing

dead: shocked lunar scree's blackout of
alpenglow—a lonely outback overhead,
a dome each nameless star's nailed in!

Streaked craters razed by scars, monsoons'
melee, splotched skin of crusted knuckles
struck; flood plains shucked raw & balked,

bald boulders smashed to rut as over
us we've discerned a chance-slant star
erupt, which falls across the scattered

heavens leaking damaged light. Like a match-
book in which each head holds a secret flame
inside its cover and loves nothing but to think

of being itched, that meteor now ruptures on
air's quick-strike fuse. Above, we catch this far-
flung rock let loose. A stunned line burning up.

Home Truths

Homecoming

My kid brother, Josh, who's 28 years old, still lives
at home and works at Wal-Mart, the graveyard shift
to earn an extra buck—without insurance, a pinch

less than 40 hours. Each week he's stuck within
the shuffle. His flipflopped part-time schedule brings
him back on Sundays, where he punches in, hopped up.

He wishes he could turn it down, turn back to sleep.
He needs to take a load off, but instead he off-loads
shipping crates, price-guns invoice, cancels breakage,

stacks up stock, pulls liquor from a locker, takes peanuts
out from boxes. Shelving, he ignores the expiration dates
before he sneaks a 15-minute break for lunch—dinner—

whatever you'd call Pop Tarts, Red Bull, and a protein shake
scarfed down between two cigarettes. He sees the same Day-
Glo façade of strip malls with their aisles of ricocheting light,

alone within a prefab big-box crater where he loses sight
of anything except the whitewashed walls and an overhead
twitch of fluorescent luster, before he punches out, freefalls

fast asleep, climbing in a hatchback with his girlfriend
of the week. Awake, she nudges him; they kiss. She drops
him off. His drooping eyes no match for staring down

the clock. He boosts some painkillers, punching out.
I pick him up this time; he boasts *I should be proud,
not everyone's the brother of the Son of God.* What

kind of crap is that? But then he crazy-talks about
infinity's a maze of circles. C'mon, nobody's stuck on earth.
End times are almost over. I'm raptured into some divinity—

he faces the lit-up runway of Dover Air Force Base.
You must have faith, we'll all be judged by our good works.
I ask him why he hasn't quit? *Fuck, you think*

I haven't tried? Not buying it, he rolls up his sleeve:
a new tattoo dyed royal. *A present to myself. Damned*
near killed me, too. I turned into a zombie. Face blue enough

to match my collar. Needles at the shop delivered shell-
fish residue into my blood. Soon shocked my system.
Dragged ass to work, but they sent me back for once,

saying I'd scare away their customers. Felt like a heart
attack for two-three days while drifting off, seeing stars,
and barely knowing I was there enough to half-believe

there might be any world still reeling beyond the end of me . . .
A scar's since shriveled up my arm. Hardly like I'd been
out huffing, but mom and dad got pissed when I went off

to party. But hey, we're born to suffer for our will to live.
Later, I argue with my parents. How could they
miss the warning signs? A shrink looks at him,

sends him upstate to the mental ward. Giving up
all drink and pills, he starts to think more clearly,
and sees a hole he's dug himself and can't afford

to backfill. He assumes an attitude of some working
stiff; resumes his makeshift grind. But my brother's
warped tattoo proclaims, "Mad 4 Life," no kidding.

My hometown

Camden, Delaware

became the sprawl it's crotched between,
all shaved golf courses, rich damp swamps,
strip malls along Highway 13

with billboards promising the pomp
of beach resorts if you head south
past vacant trailer-parks Duchamp

could not redeem; tract homes without
one soul around to buy them, lawns
parched colorless as sauerkraut.

Sky raptured with synthetic dawn,
buzzkilling spray from single-prop
biplanes above gaunt barns from bygone

days. Chain buffets with tater-tots
and self-serve meats ensure the taste is
all you can stomach, cold or hot.

High grass grows over rusted chassis
on lawns of rednecks, who bum-rush
bald tires at the NASCAR races.

Like liquor stores, in easy reach,
big churches next to empty shops;
foreclosures on the nouveau riche.

Yet still they till the latest crop,
more low-rent chain stores with obscene
vast acreage of their cracked blacktops.

Mayday

Again, I'm standing in this vacant field,
the boxy subdivision behind my house,
its marshy ground unfit for septic, feeble
with my own dull grief, a porch-lit sense
of wasted years—of how we're all kept strung
along with promises while doubtful hope
fades out like terror-ruined light. Just staring
at the rocks, as if their lichen plastered maps
on four blank walls inside my brain: I yearn
for lightning's manuscript, that quick first sip,
that giddy drag which turns into a pack-
a-day. I hike out past Virginia creeper,
the slick green cesspit of the motel pool,
which bobbles with old cigarettes and empty
bottles—the liquor store already closed;
a muculent and jewel-bright drifting shuck
of trucks along the interstate. The surf,
as each one barrels by, would lift my name
and strip it to a curse. I float beneath
the fireflies, cell tower lights, whatever stars
descend: a shade wrapped in its cerement.
I've traded half my life to end up here,
a peeling billboard pleading Rent This Space.
Its floodlights blister where shrill bugs ferment
and boil in the foiled, not-quite-summer air—
this urge and urge through numbered days,
some wished-for but never-satisfied intake
of breath. Each parceled lot, each busted stop

sign, rusted wire, raw litter spilled, it's all
gulped down as if a pill. Alone, I walk
beside my thinning shadow, remembering chance
links between the words I'm playing. Telephone
lines knock with knots of stolen bowling shoes.
One pole's been stapled with a missing face:
rain-soaked, sun-wasted ink that runs and splotches.
I wonder for a moment if it's mine.

Addiction

The glare squints back, nothing but stalled cars.
You're heading for the bar, to get picked up or
pick a fight, after hours brooding on the voids

and expirations, busting ass over boosted inventory
or breakage, noodling about—makeshift, gassed—
at Wal-Mart before you've lumbered off to Lowe's,

bored thick enough to build an ark. This double
toil done took its toll, a life all highs and lows.
By noon, you're like an arctic wolf—could lick

a greasy knife, ice-numb, until your tongue is blood.
Snuffling the house, you'd down the neon mouth-
wash to its last sweet drop. Red pills you've boosted

rattle in your brain. Still, you've absorbed enough
philosophy from films and tried to make an art
from sorrows in the lower depths, so twelve-step

to it: stop, adjust—change your life—touch
the rough, raw skins that hold your body in;
unroll one last pure nub of stubbed-out ash.

Keep hoarding Buffalo nickels for a ticket out.
But you shuffle back, no sleep for second shift;
lickety-split, each buck you make disintegrates.

Your collages like mirages of the lapsing heavens
you see inside your funk. Its starlight raptures off
the off-white walls. You rub out the sun. Junkbook

auras. Fallout, jism, black holes, benders. Pipedreams
warpspeed into smoke and mirrors. Find a girl to toss
those loaded dice, your pared-down pried-out wisdom

teeth. You hope to get hitched up as if some bride might
save you. How many rings you've lost that way, each
link in one long chain. You need a drink. You're stuck

in traffic, though. Lodged athwart the median's
panicgrass, a stranded rattletrap billows darkly.
No reason, this seedy Dodge bursts into flames.

Half Sister

She went to intern at the vet's,
surrounded by the empty cages.
She glanced at shows or books, depending
on if ads beckoned or a pet
scraped at its dish. She turned the pages
on which she doodled half-pretending . . .

No one seemed to know my sister.
Eventually, she went away
to college, then she transferred back
and lived at home to finish her
last term. Soon buried in the day-
to-day of her new job, its black

and white, measuring control
groups, nervous rabbits, red-eyed mice,
recording their slow side-effects.
She fast adjusted to her role,
sterile lab coat and the precise
split-dosage schedule to inject;

the rows of vials, double-blind,
exposure levels, routines for detox,
discarding of the biohazards.
Go in early, work overtime,
weekends on call, and beat the clock.
With time each detail can be mastered.

No surprises, no room for error;
spacious townhouse, lives near the beach.
A morning run, all she can muster.
Keep saving up. Whole closets for
more clothes from Gap; knickknacks in niches . . .
I know nothing of my sister.

Crop Cycle

Crop dusters spray fluorescent clouds, then turn,
swoop low, and dribble off their mist.
My notebooks scribbled over broken fields;
I walk daylong returning home.

I've stood a shadow in the meadow's sway.
All air: stale words I've breathed before.
A gnomon wheeling under circled hawks,
I am what darkens in each grain.

Small manor's furrows blotted with manure
endure to rot, as dust smooths dust
and rusted teeth seal shut on shot machines.
Estranged remembering the old

stale pasture growing past its greening swale,
I dreamt that meaning failed each fold.
My pleas are swallowed by a quiet breeze.
Topsoil's held by nothing's root.

A country's heart of maize where history's lost,
the watersheds bank pesticides
and eat away the land they drain across,
clear syrups we all have subsidized.

The soybean farmers must book every seed
big agra sells them back. While crows
caw out and gag as if they wore a noose,
their wings drag shade across my form.

More poison drifting from the planes, this house
soon splinters in the noonday sun.
A cloud pursued by wind pursued by cloud's
a fog no center can arrange.

Haunting

My father was adept at making masks.
Each Halloween he'd give himself the task
to fashion from the castoff cardboard boxes
at his factory a costume to outfox
the routine drag. But not for him, for me.
He'd work it like an armor till it ceded
an armadillo, damselfly, or lobster.
A mobster's lair or a secret lab—
pink packing peanuts filled our living room.
What fantasy this year would I assume
once he had wrinkled, pasted, patched, and painted
in labor those long nights alone with pained
expressions of pure pleasure? Ah, my inkling
was a furtive cockroach with hairy, gangling
arms I'd puppet up as light as rags
and close like one tight fist. But no, a daddy
longlegs took shape from all those shipping crates.
At the parade, the whole contraption weighed
down my shoulders; a visor's compound eyes
fit snug upon my cranium, the size
of hand-me-downs too small and big at once,
which crushed me like ten pounds for every ounce.
What we inherit, we must make our own,
says Goethe. Stitched-up heads and broken bones
and Frankensteined spare parts abound. I pass
a sea of nasty children posing as
trolls, werewolves, witches, fairies, babies, ghosts.
I search for Father but I fear he's lost
since every frozen visage looks like his,
blank mirrors of the self's paralysis
which I've projected toddling through the crowd,

shoved back by ghouls, pushed forward by the clowns.
Then goaded on, I find him. He says we won
most terrifying. Pandemonium
of seeing oneself, stripped of one's façades,
a spider dangled from the hands of god.
He rarely said a word but showed his love
in rougher ways I'd guess the meanings of,
such as when pressing me to peel my costume
off—shell in which I'd never feel accustomed . . .
Traditions grip us with estranging force.

A man is the collection of his faces.

Fatalist

Winds change or change your knack,
I've told my brother, take
heart, don't pursue bad veins
of thought. But times are lean,

and winds keep getting knocked
right out of him. He's ticked,
and starting to revive
mistakes from which he learns

nothing. His face gets nicked.
His half-clean shirt's untucked.
"No use," he says, "it's vain—
I'll drink and die: alone."

He nibbles bones he's nuked,
whatever meat's intact.
Nobody intervenes
when he begs, "Another loan."

He grabs keys off the nook,
jumps smack into the truck.
He's off. It's déjà vu.
What drives him like a loon?

Midnight, he tramps half-naked
past alleyways through tricks
of light, thick looping vines
that hassle vacant lanes.

My brother lays his neck
upon the railroad track
and baffles far-out vibes
that tremor down the line.

Double Dutch

A beaded rope claps off the ground,
another loops back in reverse—

the blacktop tapped, each city block
gray brickwork down which they have tripped.

The checkered projects fade away.
A tree nearby has dropped its leaves,

fruit scraping on the cracked-up road.
A trap is set; the troop counts off:

a girl has stepped inside an egg,
which swoops and snaps

below her legs, above her head,
so many forces gyroscope

as they rehearse to face them out—
each foot floats over shadow's fate

and skips and scats with every twist
avoiding double-time and faster

tricks, the counter-slap
she pivots out of with a practiced

stagger, having learned the ropes;
slips under this still-spinning braid

to hand it off. Another girl quick-
leaping in, lopes on her toes—

a swing that threatens broken yolks,
the noise around her keeping up

this game with time she's kept by, still
remembering to evade each turn.

Terminal

The Greyhound downshifts to a chuffed-out grind.
A shock of lights awake the eyes of strangers
who've slumped on one another's shoulders, rolled
across three states, holding duffels in their laps,
their temples rattled on hard panes of glass.
They grab their jumbled packs from overhead
and shuffle off, vegetal, out the gate,
late stumble down a crumbling street to harbor
or a slumber through dark tunnels into slums,
to Meadowlands beyond these storied heights.
I left a girl and job, almost a life
ago. The holidays over, I'm going back home.
Yeah, missed connection. 11:20's
last chance to transfer, so a gaunt white cop
has grumbled. Can't sleep in Port Authority.
Best get a room. Six sharp, the first bus leaves.
I hoist the deadweight of my lumpy bag,
avoid the shit-stained bum crouched on the floor,
and figure I can find an after-hours
dive nearby, which leaves me with some time
to kill. I wander up 9th Avenue
until I find a godforsaken hole-
in-the-wall—it's all rubble, plywood, braces
between two dumps beneath some overpass.
The bartender, in a lacy bra and cut-
offs which show a little sag of ass, ignores
me. I gork onto a stool. Another man down
the end is cradling his face inside
the crook of his locked arms; comes up to smoke,
giving me the eye. A drunk keeps punching
buttons on the busted juke and feeding it

more coins while someone else adjusts a radio.
Half-smudged, "Our Specal Deal 2nite is: Shot."
I see the man beyond the mirror's end
is blind—the clock I've studied hasn't moved
in days. There's nothing here that works, but all
pay dues somehow as if they owed a debt
of gratitude to forces that have kept
them up this long. When last call comes, I pitch
outside and breathe the ruddy smear of dawn
by the transport depot with its sweet exhaust;
I feel each minute drain away the stars.

Pay Phone

I still recall those lovers' hands
that gripped me tight, their mouths pressed close, ecstatic,
days I was a Laocoön of twisting limbs and
    a breathless pulse of static—

now, sticky, busted, sprayed, and spewed
with tags nearby some underpass I stand
filled up with apple cores, gum-wrappers, residues
    as if a garbage can

or upright, coffin-sized dropbox.
A businessman who buzzes by refuses
me a glance, whips his touch-screen iPhone out that mocks
    my tangled, earthbound muse:

my book—once thick with every name
that spells the rendezvous of city blocks—
gets minced to pulp. My folding door, which someone's jammed
    a flyer in, is locked;

the symbols rubbed until they're gone
along my pad, each key almost remains
a mangled hieroglyph like the Rosetta Stone.
    Dangling off the hook, I am

no more a hot bed for erratic
counterfeits in encounters fit for one
who hangs on every word and pumps spare change in quick
    before the dial-tone.

Troubled Kid

I ride the cheese bus home, a raucous mess
of kids all mouthing off. With one seat left,
I sit next to this punk with zits and pit-stains,
rattail, his backpack poking in my ribs. He smells
like paint thinner and onion rings; stares vacantly
past a window wiped with Dungeons & Dragons
symbols along with what I think are swastikas
beyond which I can view white lumps of soot-
caked snowbanks in the shadows, yellow patches
above the septic tanks, junker cars on blocks.
Everything canceled like the skeletons of trees.
I've seen him shuffle down the hall at school
with a ragged pack of hicks to Special Ed.
Some girl once whispered that the kid's disturbed.
I level with him, saying, Quit touching me.
He laughs and shakes his head before glancing back
toward another trailer park, a stray dog in the street,
then pinches my left leg. I slap his hand away.
He glares at me, and looks like he's about to spit,
but punches while I dodge so it just hits my arm.
Fuck off, I say. Words seldom on my lips.
He elbows me again. I'm livid, silent.
I scoot away; write in my civics journal.
A few minutes pass. I think it's maybe over
when he turns around and rips my page in two.
That's when I plunge my pencil in his thigh
then grab a fist of hair and smash his head
into the windowpane. I keep it up. I keep it up.

A gash of blood seeps over foggy glass.
The driver stops the bus. She kicks me off.
She calls my parents to come pick me up.
I sicken in my guts and cuss him out.
Thick flurries sticking fast, I shudder, huddle,
watch taillights through exhaust, my breath a plume
which makes quicksilver figures through the cold.
I hold a greasy tuft inside my palm . . .
Flash-forward three years later. Another winter,
I ride that same old bus, an awkward freshman,
fidgety and glum. A folded note gets slipped
onto my seat: a clipped-out, wrinkled photo
from the daily obit—his face half-smiles back,
half-shrinks away while squinting into sun.
An older kid leans in and smirks, Rumor is
he took his father's gun, the poor doomed jerk,
and shot himself straight in the mouth.

Brother's Keeper

Each day's a nonstop starting over:
every morning's on-the-mend is

a renewal of that originary promise.
My brother, if not quite sober,

will be dazzled by the sunlight,
which he'll likely misconstrue—

stepping quick & loose
from the hospital, his sprightly,

lank limbs scarred & freckled
& tattooed—for insubstantial angels.

Past fence, past weed, past tangle,
he caroms into the wreck

he's made his life. Numbers
razzled in some damaged thesis:

he's proved to me he's Jesus
between another swig & stumble

times we've discussed his math until
he's cussed me. No one can police

his fallen faith or leaps of love. Released,
no one now can hold him. Against his will

ripe wheatfields sway & stalk between us
as if it's time to rotate once again

the same gray arid ground. Late summer grains
infuse each tipping head at dusk.

I look behind his eyes into his face
& watch a shockwave off one bullet

riddle sunflicked motes' dream-slow ballet.
I fix myself for his embrace.

Inclemency

These latter days I'd rather hide my face
with eavesdroppers and scopophiliacs
who've taken shelter in this musty dive.

Boy, just lookee at that rain and hail.
Woo-wee, sugar! Scatter, brain matter,
and the weather's gray from ear to ear:

a great big blinding flash! Now I count
down to thunder but it never comes,
which means the lightning's right smack

dab inside my head—amid the bluff
analysis, loyalty to failures, sawdust,
logic's cannibals, and balled-up scraps

of cash. It's raw and cloudy like the out-
line of a candled egg, this facsimile that's
been over-copied into smutch. Exactly so,

I'm getting hammered; the chips are down.
Shadows drink their bodies up then slip
away. Everyone out there is saying *cheese*.

And me, me or the demiurge, being half
the source of all I sense, am still not sold
each detail's burnt into a verge with fact.

Origin

Expect delays. Roadblocks, back roads. Snow-blind
heaps and drifts. Lines of tumbled traffic cones.
Deer leaping in your lane. Wind-twisted signs
for detours out. Abandoned mobile homes . . .

The crumbs I've followed come from my old shoes.
Doors swing foreclosed. I peel away my face
as if a longneck's label, hangnails, loose
ends—so much dead skin I've written off, unfazed.

The blizzard whistles sing-alongs. It's on repeat.
Whiteouts. Black ice. You say I should embrace
mistakes. But I refrain. I turn down one-way streets.
I'm washed with the weather. You fade into space.

Will Cordeiro has work published in *Agni, Best New Poets, The Cincinnati Review, Copper Nickel, The Offing, DIAGRAM, Poetry Northwest, Threepenny Review, THRUSH Poetry Journal*, and elsewhere. Will coedits the small press Eggtooth Editions and is grateful for a grant from the Arizona Commission on the Arts, a scholarship from Sewanee Writers' Conference, and a Truman Capote Writer's Fellowship, as well as residencies from ART 342, Blue Mountain Center, Ora Lerman Trust, Petrified Forest National Park, and Risley Residential College. Will received an MFA and PhD from Cornell University. Will is also coauthor of *Experimental Writing: A Writer's Guide and Anthology*, forthcoming from Bloomsbury. Currently, Will lives in Flagstaff and teaches in the Honors College at Northern Arizona University.

ALSO FROM ABLE MUSE PRESS

Jacob M. Appel, *The Cynic in Extremis: Poems*

William Baer, *Times Square and Other Stories; New Jersey Noir: A Novel; New Jersey Noir (Cape May): A Novel; New Jersey Noir (Barnegat Light): A Novel*

Lee Harlin Bahan, *A Year of Mourning (Petrarch): Translation*

Melissa Balmain, *Walking in on People (Able Muse Book Award for Poetry)*

Ben Berman, *Strange Borderlands: Poems; Figuring in the Figure: Poems*

David Berman, *Progressions of the Mind: Poems*

Lorna Knowles Blake, *Green Hill (Able Muse Book Award for Poetry)*

Michael Cantor, *Life in the Second Circle: Poems*

Catherine Chandler, *Lines of Flight: Poems*

William Conelly, *Uncontested Grounds: Poems*

Maryann Corbett, *Credo for the Checkout Line in Winter: Poems; Street View: Poems; In Code: Poems*

Brian Culhane, *Remembering Lethe: Poems*

John Philip Drury, *Sea Level Rising: Poems*

Rhina P. Espaillat, *And After All: Poems*

Anna M. Evans, *Under Dark Waters: Surviving the* Titanic: *Poems*

Stephen Gibson, *Frida Kahlo in Fort Lauderdale: Poems*

D. R. Goodman, *Greed: A Confession: Poems*

Carrie Green, *Studies of Familiar Birds: Poems*

Margaret Ann Griffiths, *Grasshopper: The Poetry of M A Griffiths*

Janis Harrington, *How to Cut a Woman in Half: Poems*

Katie Hartsock, *Bed of Impatiens: Poems*

Elise Hempel, *Second Rain: Poems*

Jan D. Hodge, *Taking Shape: Carmina figurata; The Bard & Scheherazade Keep Company: Poems*

Ellen Kaufman, *House Music: Poems*

Len Krisak, *Say What You Will (Able Muse Book Award for Poetry)*

Emily Leithauser, *The Borrowed World (Able Muse Book Award for Poetry)*

Hailey Leithauser, *Saint Worm: Poems*

Carol Light, *Heaven from Steam: Poems*

Kate Light, *Character Shoes: Poems*

April Lindner, *This Bed Our Bodies Shaped: Poems*

Martin McGovern, *Bad Fame: Poems*

Jeredith Merrin, *Cup: Poems*

Richard Moore, *Selected Poems; The Rule That Liberates: An Expanded Edition: Selected Essays*

Richard Newman, *All the Wasted Beauty of the World: Poems*

Alfred Nicol, *Animal Psalms: Poems*

Deirdre O'Connor, *The Cupped Field (Able Muse Book Award for Poetry)*

Frank Osen, Virtue, *Big as Sin (Able Muse Book Award for Poetry)*

Alexander Pepple (Editor), *Able Muse Anthology;*
    Able Muse: A Review of Poetry, Prose & Art (semiannual, winter 2010 on)

James Pollock, *Sailing to Babylon: Poems*

Aaron Poochigian, *The Cosmic Purr: Poems; Manhattanite (Able Muse Book Award for Poetry)*

Tatiana Forero Puerta, *Cleaning the Ghost Room: Poems*

Jennifer Reeser, *Indigenous: Poems; Strong Feather: Poems*

John Ridland, *Sir Gawain and the Green Knight (Anonymous): Translation;*
    Pearl (Anonymous): Translation

Stephen Scaer, *Pumpkin Chucking: Poems*

Hollis Seamon, *Corporeality: Stories*

Ed Shacklee, *The Blind Loon: A Bestiary*

Carrie Shipers, *Cause for Concern (Able Muse Book Award for Poetry)*

Matthew Buckley Smith, *Dirge for an Imaginary World (Able Muse Book Award for Poetry)*

Susan de Sola, *Frozen Charlotte: Poems*

Barbara Ellen Sorensen, *Compositions of the Dead Playing Flutes: Poems*

Rebecca Starks, *Time Is Always Now: Poems; Fetch Muse: Poems*

Sally Thomas, *Motherland: Poems*

J.C. Todd, *Beyond Repair: Poems*

Paulette Demers Turco (Editor), *The Powow River Poets Anthology II*

Rosemerry Wahtola Trommer, *Naked for Tea: Poems*

Wendy Videlock, *Slingshots and Love Plums: Poems;*
    The Dark Gnu and Other Poems; Nevertheless: Poems

Richard Wakefield, *A Vertical Mile: Poems; Terminal Park: Poems*

Gail White, *Asperity Street: Poems*

Chelsea Woodard, *Vellum: Poems*

Rob Wright, *Last Wishes: Poems*

www.ablemusepress.com

CPSIA information can be obtained
at www.ICGtesting.com
Printed in the USA
LVHW092100100421
684118LV00002B/36